Ancient Civilizations

Published by Creative Education
P.O. Box 227, Mankato, Minnesota 56002
Creative Education is an imprint of
THE CREATIVE COMPANY
www.thecreativecompany.us

Design and production by CHRISTINE VANDERBEEK
Art direction by RITA MARSHALL

Printed in the United States of America

PHOTOGRAPHS BY Alamy (Michal Boubin, Danita
Delimont, Peter Horree, Image Source, Picturebank,
Robert Harding Picture Library Ltd), Corbis (Historical
Picture Archive, National Geographic Society, Gianni
Dagli Orti, Robert Harding World Imagery, Ivan
Vdovin/JAI, Roger Wood), Shutterstock (Rachelle
Burnside, jsp, Dudarev Mikhail, Waj), SuperStock
(Corbis, DeAgostini, Fine Art Images)

LIBRARY OF CONGRESS
CATALOGING-IN-PUBLICATION DATA
Bodden, Valerie.
Egypt / Valerie Bodden.
p. cm. — (Ancient civilizations)
Includes bibliographical references and index.
SUMMARY: A historical overview of the Egyptian civiliza-
tion from the perspectives of the social classes, from the
king to the laborers, including the North African king-
doms' growth and decline.

ISBN 978-1-60818-392-0
1. Egypt—Civilization—to 332 B.C.—Juvenile literature.
I. Title.

DT61.B596 2014
932'.01—dc23   2013032512

ccss: RI.5.1, 2, 3, 5, 6, 8, 9; RH.6-8.4, 5, 6, 7, 8, 9

FIRST EDITION
9 8 7 6 5 4 3 2 1

CREATIVE ◆ EDUCATION

EGYPT

VALERIE BODDEN

Egypt

TABLE OF CONTENTS

INTRODUCTION

The Nile River flows from south to north through the land of Egypt, bringing life to the narrow strips of land alongside its banks. It was on that river that one of the world's first great civilizations arose. People first settled along the Nile in Egypt more than 9,000 years ago. Over time, these settlers came together to form small towns and villages. Those towns and villages, in turn, joined together into larger units, until Egypt consisted of two kingdoms: Lower Egypt in the north and Upper Egypt in the south. According to tradition, a ruler from Upper Egypt named Narmer (or Menes) conquered Lower Egypt and united the two kingdoms around 3100 B.C. He established a civilization that would flourish for the next

The winding Nile River attracted ancient peoples to its waters and fertile banks.

nearly 3,000 years.

Those 3,000 years were marked by alternating periods of unity and disunity. Historians have given each period a unique name. From Egypt's unification until the building of the first pyramids around 2575 B.C. is the time known as the Early Dynastic Period. This was followed by the Old Kingdom (2575–2130 B.C.), during which Egypt's greatest pyramids were built. By the end of the Old Kingdom, Egypt's government had weakened, leading to the First Intermediate Period (2130–1938 B.C.), when a number of rulers claimed to be king simultaneously. The Middle Kingdom (1938–1630 B.C.) was marked by a strong, centralized government, but it eventually collapsed. During the Second Intermediate Period (1630–1540 B.C.), peoples from southwest Asia known as the Hyksos, or "foreign kings," took power in Egypt. After the Hyksos were

EGYPT CIRCA 1479 B.C.

expelled around 1540 B.C., Egypt entered a period known as the New Kingdom, which marked the height of its power and wealth. By about 1075 B.C., the New Kingdom came to an end as outside powers began to overtake Egypt's territory.

Even as Egypt's government went through periods of dominance and decline, the kingdom's social structure remained remarkably stable. At the top of Egyptian society was the ruler. Below him was a small group of literate officials who held government offices, served in the priesthood, and led the military. The majority of the population served as laborers on farms or in workshops. Few Egyptians ever moved out of the social class into which they were born. Beginning in the Middle Kingdom, however, there were occasional instances of people born into lower-class families rising to some of the highest positions in the land.

The pyramids of ancient Egypt are human-made marvels providing us insight into the past.

PALACES, PYRAMIDS, AND PHARAOHS

Today, we usually refer to the kings of ancient Egypt as pharaohs. But this term was not commonly used until about 1400 B.C. Instead, Egyptian kings went by a series of titles that indicated their position as an earthly god and the absolute ruler of Egypt. A pharaoh had almost unlimited power, serving as the head of government as well as chief priest and head of the military.

A pharaoh's power was reflected in his special clothing. A bull's tail hung from the back of his pleated skirt, indicating that he was as strong as a bull. In addition, he wore a headdress adorned with the image of a rearing cobra to symbolize the goddess

The cobra, called a uraeus, on an Egyptian pharaoh's headdress served as a warning to enemies.

Wadjet, who was believed to protect him. Some pharaohs also carried a full leopard skin, including the head, across their shoulders. A long, false beard hung from a pharaoh's chin, and he carried a crook and a *flail*. In his presence, commoners had to lie flat, while nobles knelt and touched their heads to the ground. No one could speak to the pharaoh unless granted permission.

A pharaoh could generally marry whomever he wanted, and most pharaohs had several wives. A pharaoh's chief wife might be his half-sister (the daughter of his father and a different mother). Lesser wives might come from Egypt's elite families. Pharaohs often also married foreign princesses to secure political alliances with other nations or rulers.

When a pharaoh died, the throne generally went to the oldest son of his chief wife. On some occasions, however, the sons of lesser wives were crowned pharaoh. Other male relatives might also succeed to the throne, sometimes on the basis of an appointment by the former pharaoh or a religious *oracle*. Pharaohs who had no sons might appoint high-ranking government officials to succeed them. Military commanders also sometimes came to power upon the death of a pharaoh.

Did You Know?

THE GREAT PYRAMID

OF GIZA WAS THE

LARGEST PYRAMID EVER

BUILT, ORIGINALLY

MEASURING 481 FEET

(147 M) HIGH.

Scholars believe that Egypt may have been ruled by female leaders on four different occasions. One of the most significant was Hatshepsut, who ruled for her husband's young son. Hatshepsut adopted many of the physical signs and symbols of a male pharaoh, including the false beard.

Egyptian pharaohs controlled nearly all the wealth—as well as most of the land—in Egypt. And they stuck much of that wealth into building huge palaces for themselves. Palaces were generally made of mud brick. Palace complexes might have a building for the pharaoh as well as separate areas for his wives, his children, and his royal guards. There was also a kitchen, a festival hall, stables, and a man-made lake. Floors were often decorated with images of flowers and animals to represent the earth.

A huge staff served the pharaoh and his family at the palace. Kitchen staff, groundskeepers, and carpenters ensured that the palace was kept running smoothly. Other workers took care of the pharaoh's appearance and health. The pharaoh had his own royal hairdresser, royal

A temple honoring Queen Hatshepsut was built into the cliffs off the Nile's west bank.

barber, and royal bathers. A royal sandalbearer took care of the pharaoh's shoes, while a chief washer washed his clothes. Royal doctors attended to any physical concerns. When the pharaoh left the palace, he might take 50 or more people with him, including **sedan** carriers, fan bearers, and bodyguards.

Even as a pharaoh focused on the comforts of this life, he spent even more time and money ensuring that he would have a comfortable afterlife. The Egyptians believed that after a pharaoh died, he would be brought back to life as a god. In order to return to life, though, the pharaoh's body needed to remain intact. Early pharaohs protected their remains by constructing rectangular tombs called *mastabas*. Below the mud-brick mastaba was a burial chamber, as well as storage chambers for the supplies the pharaoh was believed to need in his next life.

Around 2630 B.C., a pharaoh named Djoser created a more elaborate tomb. It consisted of six mastabas of decreasing size stacked on top of one another to form a step pyramid. Djoser's successors also built pyramids. Soon, the "steps" of the pyramids were filled in to create smooth, sloped sides. The greatest pyramids were built on the Giza **plateau**, near the present-day city of Cairo. The pyramids were connected to temples where offerings could be made to the pharaohs after their deaths.

Pyramids continued to serve as tombs for pharaohs through much of the Old and Middle Kingdoms. But these large structures, glinting in the sunlight across the desert, quickly became a target for grave robbers eager to snatch the jewels, gold, and other goods buried with the pharaohs. During the New Kingdom, pharaohs began to carve tombs into the limestone cliffs of the desert valley across the Nile from the city of Thebes. Eventually known as the Valley of the Kings, this desolate landscape became the site of more than 60 hidden tombs.

Like the pyramids of earlier pharaohs, the tombs in the Valley of the Kings contained numerous underground chambers. One chamber held the king's body, which had been mummified. This ensured that his body would be preserved for the afterlife. The process of mummification involved removing the organs and drying the body with natron, a kind of salt. The dried body was then wrapped in linen and placed in a sarcophagus, or stone coffin.

A pharaoh was buried with the food, clothing, and furniture he was thought to need in the afterlife. Statues of servants and soldiers also filled chambers of the pharaoh's tomb. The Egyptians believed that these statues would magically come to life to serve the pharaoh when he awoke. The walls of the chambers were covered with the words of prayers and spells known as Pyramid Texts. These were believed to contain magic that would help the pharaoh journey safely to the afterlife. There were also paintings depicting scenes of the pharaoh's life on Earth in the hope that the gods would allow him to continue to enjoy similar activities in the afterlife.

Giza tombs typically contained images of pharaohs, gods, and scenes from the Pyramid Texts.

WRITING AND RULING

The pharaoh was the ultimate authority in everything. But he could not be everywhere and do everything at once. So he employed a number of elite Egyptians to serve as government officials. These officials took care of the day-to-day business of keeping the kingdom running. They collected taxes, organized building projects, and oversaw legal disputes, among other things.

The most powerful government official—aside from the pharaoh—was the vizier. Each day, he heard reports from the government officials who oversaw public works, the treasury, the courts, and other aspects of administering the land. He then passed necessary information on to the pharaoh. The vizier also had the

Although the vizier was powerful, he took orders from the pharaoh and had to obey.

authority to appoint and dismiss officials and served as judge in important criminal cases. During the New Kingdom, the office of vizier was split into two positions, one for Upper and one for Lower Egypt.

Another important government official was the overseer of the treasury, who collected and stored tax payments. Since the ancient Egyptians did not have a monetary system, these taxes were generally paid in the form of crops and other goods and were used to provide for the royal family as well as for the tomb builders and others working on state-sponsored projects.

In addition to federal officials, the Egyptian government employed numerous local administrators. Ancient Egypt was divided into about 42 separate provinces, or *nomes*. Each nome was ruled by a governor known as a *nomarch* (*NOM-ark*). Under the nomarch were local mayors, chiefs, and councils. During Egypt's earliest periods, nearly all government officials were chosen from the royal family. Later, when Egypt was ruled by strong pharaohs, non-royal Egyptians began to be appointed to state offices. When the pharaoh's power weakened—as during the First and Second Intermediate

periods—government offices often became hereditary. This soon created a group of elite families who controlled most of the Egyptian government. Later, pharaohs appointed military officers to many government posts. No matter how they came into office, top officials were richly rewarded for their service, usually in the form of large estates.

A government official generally began his career as a scribe—someone who had been taught to read and write—and worked his way into higher offices. Thousands of scribes worked for the Egyptian government. They kept records, tracked taxes, and made notes about the pharaoh's reign. Most scribes were paid in food rations, and some might also have received a wage. Not all scribes became wealthy, but the ability to read and write set them apart from 95 percent of the Egyptian population.

In general, the position of a scribe was hereditary. Boys from elite families began their scribal training sometime between the ages of 5 and 10. Scribal schools were often held at a temple or a government department's office. Scribes taught Egypt's two writing systems: hieroglyphics and hieratic. Hieroglyphs were a series

Scribes and all other ancient Egyptians made ritual offerings to appease the gods.

SCRIBES REGULARLY

USED ABOUT 500

HIEROGLYPHS BUT HAD

TO KNOW THOUSANDS

OF OTHER SYMBOLS THAT

WERE MORE SPECIALIZED.

of pictures that represented sounds and ideas. Hieratic was a cursive form of hieroglyphics that allowed scribes to write more quickly. In order to learn these writing systems, children were expected to write and recite specific passages over and over again. Some scribes progressed to advanced lessons in mathematics and construction techniques. A complete scribal education could last up to 12 years.

For the most part, Egyptian scribes were male. A few females, especially from the royal family, may have been educated, but this was not common. Instead, girls from upper-class families learned to play the harp or other instruments, as well as how to sing and dance. Girls were generally married around the age of 12 or 14. Their main role was to have children and to oversee the operation of the home. For wealthy women, this meant managing the servants.

Despite their fairly traditional role in the home, women of ancient Egypt enjoyed more rights than women in many other ancient societies. They could own property, file lawsuits, and sign contracts. Although women generally did not participate in the government, there were rare exceptions.

Most elite men and women lived in thriving Egyptian cities such as Memphis and Thebes. Their homes were made of mud brick. A modest home might have 6 to 12 rooms, while the homes of the wealthiest could have 30 or more. Some homes, especially in crowded cities, were two stories or higher. Walls might be covered with bright murals. Some homes had an open courtyard with a garden. A stairway often led to the flat roof, where a family could gather to enjoy cool breezes. The most luxurious homes also contained private bathrooms.

Most wealthy Egyptians relied on slaves or servants for any necessary manual labor. This meant that they had plenty of time for recreation. The Nile served as the meeting place for many activities, such as sailing, rowing, fishing, and swimming. Many Egyptian couples also hunted together. Some went after aquatic birds in the marshes of the Nile *delta*, while others sought desert game such as gazelle and antelope. Later in Egypt's history, the elite hunted from moving chariots. Wrestling and boxing were other favorite pastimes for both boys and men.

The elite also enjoyed hosting and attending formal banquets, which included elaborate meals, music, and dancing girls. Men and women dined together, seated on the floor or at low, individual tables. Feasts might include several kinds of bread; meat such as beef, mutton, or fowl; vegetables; and fruit. In addition, there was wine—a drink reserved for the elite.

Like the pharaoh, members of the elite class dedicated much of their wealth to constructing tombs. Some even built small pyramids. Others cut their tombs from the rock or were buried in mastabas. Wealthy Egyptians were mummified after death, and their tombs contained supplies for the afterlife as well as wall paintings depicting favorite activities.

Egyptian scribes carved hieroglyphs into tablets, coffins, furniture, walls, and monuments.

SERVANTS OF THE GODS

The pharaoh was the head of not only the government but also of religion. He was the high priest for the entire country and was expected to maintain the goodwill of the gods for the people. The Egyptians worshiped so many gods at so many temples, however, that it was impossible for the pharaoh to perform all priestly functions. So numerous priests served as his representatives.

The ancient Egyptians frequently added to the list of gods they worshiped. By the beginning of the New Kingdom, more than 1,000 gods were believed to control Egypt's fate. Most gods took the form of an animal or a being made up of parts from several animals. Some were pictured as humans or had a human body with an

Ramses II ordered temples sculpted into Abu Simbel's ancient cliffs to honor the sun gods.

animal's head. Among the greatest of the gods were the sun god Ra; Osiris, the god of the dead; and Osiris's wife Isis, the goddess of motherhood.

The Egyptians believed that everything in the world was controlled by the gods. Although the gods were generally kind, specific rituals had to be carried out in order to please them so that they would allow Egypt to prosper. These religious rituals were carried out by the priests, without the involvement of the common people.

During the Old Kingdom, priests for many of Egypt's major temples came from the royal family. Smaller local temples were generally headed by local government officials. As with government offices, priests were appointed by the pharaoh when the government was centralized. When it was decentralized, many priesthoods became hereditary. Until the New Kingdom, most priests held other government positions as well. They served in the temple for one month, then had three months off. During the New Kingdom, the office of the priesthood gained more importance, and professional priests began to work in the temples full-time.

At each temple, one priest was appointed

as "first god's servant," or chief priest. Beneath him were *wab* priests, or "pure priests." They maintained physical purity by bathing twice a day and twice a night, shaving their entire bodies and heads, and avoiding foods such as pork, fish, and beans. They wore only white linen robes and **papyrus** sandals. Other priests, known as *sem* priests, took part in special funeral ceremonies. They wore robes made of leopard skins and might shave their hair, sometimes leaving a strip on the right side of the head.

Female priestesses from the elite class were fairly common during the Old and Middle Kingdom. Most served Hathor, the goddess of the sky, women, and fertility. By the New Kingdom, few women served as priestesses any longer, but many continued to serve as musicians, singers, or dancers in the temples.

The chief duty of any priest or priestess was to serve a god or goddess at his or her temple. These temples were believed to be the homes of the gods, and the Egyptians put much time and money into building them. While homes—and even palaces—were built of mud brick, most temples were built of stone, which would continue to stand long after mud-brick structures

Guarding its temple entrance, the Great Sphinx's body likely symbolized the pharaoh's power.

WITH SO MANY WIVES,

PHARAOHS OFTEN

HAD MANY CHILDREN;

RAMSES THE GREAT

(REIGNED 1279–1213 B.C.)

HAD MORE THAN 100.

had crumbled. Most temples consisted of a large, open courtyard, a **colonnaded** hall, chambers for offerings, and an inner sanctuary. While anyone could enter the outer court of a temple, only the pharaoh and certain priests could step into the inner sanctuary. This is where the cult image, or statue, of the temple's god was kept. The cult image was usually made of bronze and decorated with gold and silver. It could be up to two feet (61 cm) tall.

It was the priests' job to take care of the cult image every day. Early in the morning, they opened the inner sanctuary and offered prayers to the statue. Then they cleaned it and clothed it in white linen. Three times a day, they presented the image with offerings of food and wine. At the end of the day, the priests closed the statue back into its sanctuary for the night.

Most ordinary Egyptians never saw the cult image, unless they attended a religious festival. Festivals were held several times throughout the year for various occasions. Some celebrated the beginning of the annual flooding of the Nile. For other festivals, the priests carried the cult images out of the seclusion of their temples to visit other gods at other temples. If such a trip involved travel on the Nile, the high priest and pharaoh might make offerings to the god while aboard a boat. Along the shore, the Egyptian people would gather to watch the boat, while some played the harp or drums and others danced. Festivals often lasted several days and involved lavish feasts, games such as tug-of-war and wrestling, and the acting out of ancient myths.

Sometimes, the participants in a festival might also have an opportunity to seek an oracle, or ask a question of a god. The god was placed in a shrine carried on the priests' shoulders. To give the god's answer, the priests moved its shrine toward the correct written response. Questions asked of the gods might be in regard to a minor decision, such as when to plant a field. In some cases, a cult statue was consulted in legal cases. The pharaoh turned to oracles when determining military strategy and political appointments.

Instead of serving at temples dedicated to the gods, some priests served in mortuary temples. These were dedicated to a dead king or other wealthy person. Mortuary priests took part in the deceased's funeral ceremony. Afterward, they ensured that offerings of food and other goods were brought to the temple for the person's afterlife.

Priests in both cult temples and mortuary temples generally received a portion of the offerings given to the temple. This made some priests very wealthy. In addition, priests received free food and drink. And because a priest was serving as a representative of pharaoh to the gods, the position brought prestige and status on Earth as well.

Many pharaohs, including Ramses II, contributed to what is now known as the Temple of Luxor.

MILITARY MIGHT

Strong natural borders kept Egypt relatively safe from invaders for much of its history. Forbidding deserts stopped enemies from the east and the west. To the north, the Mediterranean Sea separated Egypt from other lands. And in the south, the First **Cataract** of the Nile made sailing into Egypt on the river virtually impossible. Even so, the Egyptians began to raise armies as soon as the first pharaoh came to power. Early on, those armies fought off small raiding parties. Later, the army pushed Egypt's borders into the Middle East to form a large empire that included parts of present-day Syria and Palestine. These lands provided Egypt with new wealth in the form of gold, cattle, and slaves.

Ramses II ("the Great") led military expeditions throughout his reign to expand Egypt's power.

The early Egyptian army likely consisted of farmers and other Egyptians who were drafted to serve when needed. The military was organized by nomes, with each nome required to raise troops who would come together under the pharaoh's leadership. In addition to Egyptians, the army also included foreign soldiers, most of them prisoners of war from Libya and *Nubia*. These foreign soldiers often made up an elite force of archers or spearmen.

At the end of the Middle Kingdom, a group of foreign invaders known as the Hyksos took over the Egyptian government. Although they ruled Egypt for little more than a century, they left a lasting mark on the Egyptian military. The Hyksos invasion made clear the need for a permanent, professional army in Egypt. A centralized army with a distinct command structure began to take shape. The highest offices were often held by the pharaohs' sons, who led four separate military divisions named after the gods Amun, Ra, Ptah, and Seth. At the army's height, each division consisted of 5,000 soldiers. As in earlier times, much of the army was made up of foreign soldiers—sometimes they even outnumbered native Egyptian troops.

The Hyksos also introduced the Egyptians to what would become their most powerful weapon—the horse and chariot. Horses were unknown in Egypt before the Hyksos invasion, but afterward, they became a key tool in the Egyptian army. Horses pulling a chariot could move swiftly across the battlefield. Chariots also provided a safe platform from which an archer could shoot. Two soldiers generally rode on a chariot. One drove and held a shield, while the other fired arrows or threw javelins. Later, a third soldier rode along to serve as shield-bearer. The chariot corps formed the elite force of the Egyptian army. The introduction of the horse also meant that mounted soldiers could serve as mobile scouts and could then warn of enemy movements.

Horses were not the only way for soldiers to get around, though. Beginning already in the Old Kingdom, Egypt used ships on the Nile to transport troops and supplies. Although these ships formed a navy of sorts, most were not strictly dedicated to wartime efforts. The fleet appears to have carried commercial goods throughout the country as well. In addition, although soldiers rode aboard the ships, they do not seem to have trained specifically for battle at sea or on the

Egyptian ritual solar boats were made for pharaohs to journey through the afterlife.

Did You Know?

BOTH MEN AND WOMEN

IN EGYPT LINED THEIR

EYES WITH GREEN OR

BLACK MAKEUP TO

REFLECT SUNLIGHT AND

KEEP AWAY INSECTS.

river. Most often, they stood on the deck of their ship and shot arrows toward troops aboard the enemy vessel.

Early in Egypt's history, men could be called on to serve in the army when they reached the age of 20. Later, that age was likely lowered. It is possible that soldiers served for several months or a year and then had time off, while another group of soldiers did their service.

Service in the Egyptian army was not easy. Military campaigns involved long marches across the scorching desert sands. Conditions in camp were generally dirty, and there was often little food. When not on campaign, soldiers might be called on to cut or transport rock for Egypt's many building projects.

The Egyptians often timed their military campaigns for June through September, after the fields had been harvested. Since men were no longer needed to work the land, they could be called on for military service. Campaigns to Nubia in the south, however, might take place earlier or later in the year, when temperatures were milder. Egyptian archers on foot and in chariots usually opened battle by firing arrows at the enemy. The infantry then attacked, wielding spears, *maces*, battleaxes, and swords. For protection, Egyptian soldiers carried shields. Some also wore leather armor.

In addition to direct combat, the Egyptians used siege tactics, keeping an enemy city surrounded for years at a time if necessary. Enemies who failed to surrender might face total war, in which the Egyptians burned their land and deported their people. Egyptian soldiers often kept track of their kills by cutting off the hands of fallen enemies. Of course, Egyptian soldiers died in battle, too. These deaths were often eliminated from official reports of a war in order to protect the pharaoh's reputation as a perfect leader. Nevertheless, Egyptians who died in foreign lands were often carried home, where they could be buried properly.

Those soldiers who survived were amply rewarded. All soldiers received a daily allowance of bread. Some of the bread allowance could be exchanged for other goods, such as beer or cakes. These items were readily available, since bakers, brewers, and butchers accompanied the army on campaign. Commanders and high officials might receive a bread allowance 10 or 20 times greater than that of the average soldier.

While food allowances might help meet a soldier's daily needs, the more important reward was ***booty***. Soldiers often received a share of the goods—such as weapons, gold, jewelry, fabric, and horses—plundered from the enemy. They might also be given enemy prisoners to serve as their slaves. When they retired, soldiers were given plots of land. Ultimately, a successful soldier might move up through the military ranks. Army officers might also go on to enjoy a successful political career.

Egyptian women were sometimes buried with weapons, suggesting they played roles in defense or war.

PART OF THE CROWD

Although thousands of people took part in running the Egyptian government, priesthood, and military, they represented only a small fraction of Egypt's population, which was probably higher than 3 million by the New Kingdom. The majority of Egypt's people worked as farmers, but few owned the land on which they worked. Instead, the land was owned by the pharaoh, the temples, or members of the elite. Those who worked the land served as **tenant** farmers, providing most of their harvest to the landowners and the government. Although the farmers did not own the land, they probably were not free to leave it; they were obliged to continue to work it.

Egyptians developed farming techniques and utilized the Nile River for irrigation.

Thanks to the Nile, Egypt enjoyed rich farmland. Each year, the river overflowed its banks during the season of inundation (beginning around June). The flooding covered farmland with not only water but also fertile *silt*. Four months later, at the start of the season of emergence, farmers began plowing their fields and planted them with wheat, barley, or flax. The season of harvest began four months later, during which the farmers harvested and threshed their grain.

During inundation, when farmers could not work the land, many were called upon to work on the tombs and temples of the pharaohs. Some scholars believe that commoners volunteered to work on such projects, while others think workers were drafted for service. Up to 25,000 laborers may have worked on the largest pyramids at any given time. Smaller pyramids may have required a workforce of 10,000. Part of the workforce may have consisted of skilled and unskilled commoners who did not farm but were employed to work at the tombs on a permanent basis.

Permanent workers lived with their families near the tomb site in a village complete with bakeries, breweries, and homes. Temporary workers lived in camps nearby. Tomb workers received food rations and shelter as payment for their labor.

Pyramid workers were divided into groups. Some cut huge chunks of stone—weighing 2.5 tons (2.3 t) or more—from quarries. Others transported the stone to the building site, likely by ship on the Nile and then on sleds or rollers across the desert sands. Still others had to wrestle the stones into place, possibly hauling them up huge earthen ramps.

Among the workers on the tombs were skilled artists and artisans who worked as painters or sculptors. While the most skilled craftsmen were employed in tomb-making, other craftsmen toiled in workshops across Egypt. Some workshops were situated on the large estates of the wealthy. Others were sponsored by a temple or the pharaoh. A few craftsmen may have had their own small workshops.

Craft workshops turned out many objects for everyday use. Potters created vases, bowls, plates, and cups. Carpenters crafted furniture, jewelers fashioned necklaces and bracelets from precious metals and gems, and metalworkers made swords, statues, and dinnerware from copper and bronze.

Despite the fact that the upper classes needed these objects, most wealthy Egyptians looked down on craftsmen of any kind. Nearly all

Artwork on the walls of Pharaoh Seti I's tomb depicted mummies and religious rituals.

Did You Know?

SCRIBES WROTE ON

PAPYRUS WITH A BRUSH

MADE BY CHEWING ON

THE END OF A REED;

THEY DIPPED THE BRUSH

IN RED AND BLACK INK.

craftsmen remained anonymous. They never signed their works. In fact, most works were not made by a single person. Instead, individuals in a workshop were each given a single job to complete, forming a sort of assembly line. Workshop owners may have provided craftsmen with food and shelter in return for their services. Some craftsmen may have received a portion of the earnings from any goods that were sold.

Most craft jobs were held by men, but women sometimes worked as spinners, weavers, assistant bakers, or hairdressers. Some performed as singers or dancers for the wealthy. At home, women ensured that their household ran smoothly. They ground grain for making bread, cleaned the house, and cared for the children.

Few children of commoners received a formal education. Instead, they learned from their parents the skills they would need to serve as a craftsman, farmer, or homemaker. A young boy might begin working with his father by the age of 10. Girls probably began to help their mother around the house when they were seven or eight.

Like the wealthy, commoners built their homes of mud brick. But the homes of commoners were much smaller, consisting of only three or four rooms. The kitchen might be outside the house, and there was no bathroom. Some people kept animals such as donkeys or goats in the house as well.

Because of the bountiful harvests provided by the Nile, few Egyptians went hungry. But the poor ate meat less often than the rich. A single cow could cost as much as a craftsman or a farmer made in a year. Instead, commoners dined largely on bread. They also ate fruits and vegetables. Fish caught from the Nile or birds hunted in the marshes rounded out their diet.

Although most commoners were not wealthy, many employed at least a couple of servants or slaves, although the wealthy owned many more. Servants might cook, clean, care for children, or work the land. Unlike servants, who received at least a small salary, slaves worked without pay. Scholars know little about slavery in ancient Egypt. It appears that there were few slaves during Egypt's early history. During the New Kingdom, large numbers of slaves may have been drawn from those captured in war. Other slaves may have been criminals. Some people sold themselves into slavery to pay off debts. In addition, children of slave mothers automatically became slaves.

Slaves were considered property that could be bought or sold. But they did have some rights. They could own property and get married, for example. Some were treated well. Others had to perform dangerous labor in mines or quarries.

Slaves might move up the social ladder if their masters set them free. Occasionally, other commoners also improved their social standing. Some grew wealthy from their work or were recognized by the elite for their skills. Such people might eventually serve in high government positions. For most commoners, however, life continued as it always had.

Scribes captured everyday life in their records of taxes, genealogies, and stories.

END OF ANCIENT EGYPT

For more than 2,000 years, daily life in Egypt changed little. But by about 1075 B.C., Egypt had entered a period of decline marked by conflict and disunity. Beginning around 665 B.C., Egypt was conquered by the empires that surrounded it—first by Assyria, then by Persia—during the Late Period. Persian kings ruled Egypt for 200 years. Then, in 332 B.C., the ***Macedonian*** king Alexander the Great defeated the Persians and forced them out of Egypt. The Egyptians celebrated Alexander's victory and crowned him pharaoh.

After Alexander's death, his position in Egypt was taken over by one of his generals, named Ptolemy. For the next 300 years, in what came to be known as the

Alexander the Great founded Alexandria, Egypt, a center for culture and world trade.

Ptolemaic Period, Ptolemy's descendants ruled Egypt. During that time, Greek settlers took the place of the Egyptian elite in government. Egyptians who wanted to remain part of Egypt's power structure had to adopt the Greek language and culture.

The final Ptolemaic ruler was Cleopatra VII. In 30 B.C., she was defeated by the Romans, and Egypt became part of the *Roman Empire*. Although it had lost its independence, Egypt continued to have an influence over the ancient world. The Romans adopted Egyptian gods such as Isis and based aspects of their legal system on Egypt's. Even so, much of the ancient Egyptian culture was soon forgotten. Temples were abandoned, pyramids were taken apart, and tombs were robbed. Hieroglyphics fell out of use, and their meanings were forgotten.

During the European Renaissance of the 1300s through 1500s, there was a reawakening of interest in ancient Egypt. Then, in 1798,

Did You Know?

PRIESTS USED A

NILOMETER TO PREDICT

HOW HIGH NILE FLOOD-

WATERS WOULD RISE IN A

GIVEN YEAR. TAX LEVELS

WERE SET BASED ON THE

MEASUREMENTS.

Napoleon Bonaparte of France invaded Egypt. One of his soldiers discovered the Rosetta Stone, on which the same message was written in both hieroglyphics and Greek. This proved to be the key to translating hieroglyphics. Napoleon's discoveries led to a period of "Egyptomania," when people across much of the world wanted to know more about Egypt. In the 1800s, architecture, interior design, and fashion all showed signs of Egyptian influence. Another Egyptomania was sparked by the discovery of the intact tomb of King Tutankhamen in 1922.

Today, monuments from Egypt's glorious past beckon to tourists from around the world. Archaeologists continue to explore Egypt, too, hoping to uncover more of its legacy. Their findings reveal a society in which every person had his or her own role. Yet all those people came together to form the rich culture now known as ancient Egypt.

Although looked down upon by some, Egyptian farmers provided important services.

C. 7000 B.C. —	The earliest peoples live along the Nile and gradually form towns and villages, before separating into the kingdoms of Upper and Lower Egypt.
C. 3100 B.C. —	Upper and Lower Egypt are united under Narmer.
C. 3050 B.C. —	The city of Memphis is established as Egypt's capital.
C. 2630 B.C. —	Pharaoh Djoser begins the building of the first step pyramid, at Saqqara.
C. 2575 B.C. —	The Old Kingdom begins and is characterized by pyramid building.
C. 2560 B.C. —	The Great Pyramid, built for Pharaoh Khufu, is built on the Giza plateau.
C. 2345 B.C. —	Pyramid Texts begin to appear on the walls of pharaohs' tombs.
C. 2130 B.C. —	The First Intermediate Period begins, with numerous local rulers claiming to be pharaoh.
C. 2060 B.C. —	The Egyptian capital is moved to the city of Thebes.
C. 1938 B.C. —	Egypt is again united under a strong central government at the beginning of the Middle Kingdom.
C. 1630 B.C. —	The Hyksos of southwest Asia defeat Egypt and take power, introducing the horse and chariot.
C. 1540 B.C. —	The Egyptians overthrow the Hyksos, and Egypt enters a period known as the New Kingdom, during which Egypt creates an empire.
1479 B.C. —	Hatshepsut becomes coregent with Thutmose III but is also named pharaoh.
1458-25 B.C. —	Thutmose III comes to full power, and the Egyptian Empire reaches its largest extent.
C. 1075 B.C. —	The capital is moved to the city of Tanis in the Nile Delta.
C. 1075 B.C. —	Egypt enters a period of decline known as the Third Intermediate Period.
C. 665 B.C. —	Egypt during the Late Period is ruled by outsiders, including Assyria.
525 B.C. —	Persian forces conquer Egypt, and Persian kings rule for 200 years.
332 B.C. —	Alexander the Great of Macedonia conquers Egypt and is named pharaoh; he is succeeded by Ptolemy in 323 B.C.
30 B.C. —	Egypt is conquered by Rome and becomes part of the Roman Empire.

BOOTY: money or goods taken from a defeated enemy in war

CATARACT: a large waterfall or area of rapids on a river

COLONNADED: surrounded by a series of columns that are usually topped by a roof

DELTA: a low-lying, often triangle-shaped, plain of sand, gravel, and other sediment that forms between two branches of a river as it flows into the ocean

FLAIL: a farming tool made of a short stick hanging from a long wooden handle and used to separate grain from the rest of the plant

MACEDONIAN: from the ancient kingdom of Macedonia, north of Greece

MACES: heavy clubs, often with a metal end covered with spikes, that were used as weapons

NILOMETER: a column or stairway built along the banks of the Nile River that was used for measuring flood levels

NUBIA: an ancient kingdom to the south of Egypt

ORACLE: a priest or priestess through whom a god is believed to speak

PAPYRUS: a tall plant found in the Nile Valley and used to make a writing material also known as papyrus

PLATEAU: a high, flat area of land

ROMAN EMPIRE: an empire, with its capital in Rome, that ruled much of Europe, North Africa, and the Middle East from 27 B.C. to A.D. 476

SATIRE: a literary work that criticizes or makes fun of someone or something

SEDAN: a covered chair mounted on poles and carried by two people

SILT: very small pieces of sand, rock, and soil that are often carried by a moving body of water

TENANT: someone who rents a home or land from the property owner

Selected Bibliography

Brier, Bob, and Hoyt Hobbs. *Daily Life of the Ancient Egyptians*. Westport, Conn.: Greenwood Press, 2008.

Fletcher, Joann. "From Warrior Women to Female Pharaohs: Careers for Women in Ancient Egypt." BBC: History. http://www.bbc.co.uk/history/ancient/egyptians/women_01.shtml.

Kuiper, Kathleen, ed. *Ancient Egypt: From Prehistory to the Islamic Conquest*. New York: Britannica Educational Publishing, 2010.

Mertz, Barbara. *Temples, Tombs & Hieroglyphs: A Popular History of Ancient Egypt*. New York: William Morrow, 2007.

Nardo, Don. *People of the Nile: Rhythms of Daily Life*. San Diego, Calif.: Lucent, 2005.

Redford, Donald, ed. *The Oxford Encyclopedia of Ancient Egypt*. 3 vols. New York: Oxford University Press, 2001.

Romer, John. *Ancient Lives: Daily Life in Egypt of the Pharaohs*. New York: Henry Holt, 1984.

Tyldesley, Joyce. "The Private Lives of the Pyramid-Builders." BBC: History. http://www.bbc.co.uk/history/ancient/egyptians/pyramid_builders_01.shtml.

Websites

BBC HISTORY: EGYPTIANS

http://www.bbc.co.uk/history/ancient/egyptians/

Supervise the building of a pyramid, ready a body for mummification, and read letters written by ancient Egyptians.

THE BRITISH MUSEUM: ANCIENT EGYPT

http://www.ancientegypt.co.uk/menu.html

Take a virtual tour of a pyramid, sarcophagus, and temple.

Note: Every effort has been made to ensure that the websites listed above are suitable for children, that they have educational value, and that they contain no inappropriate material. However, because of the nature of the Internet, it is impossible to guarantee that these sites will remain active indefinitely or that their contents will not be altered.